The Summer of '99

To: Kristen - Sis#2
Enjoy life

December 2008

Marty J. Reeder

Outskirts Press, Inc.
Denver, Colorado

A true adventure that includes the romance of "Pay-Ree"(Paris).
Love Sherge

The Summer of '99
All Rights Reserved.
Copyright © 2008 Marty J. Reeder
V2.0

Outskirts Press, Inc.
http://www.outskirtspress.com

ISBN: 978-1-4327-2908-0

Outskirts Press and the "OP" logo are trademarks belonging to Outskirts
Press, Inc.

PRINTED IN THE UNITED STATES OF AMERICA

Train Song

Everybody knows where I'm coming from.
I don't even know where I've been.
As far as I can see, it's all left up to me
to tell you where my story begins.

Leaving on a train,
a midnight rolling train,
and I don't know if I'll be back again.

Little did I know, that home could be the road,
and now, I've made this road my friend.
It looks like I can tell, the road has done me well,
and these boots could be the way to my end.

Leaving on a train,
a midnight rolling train,
and I don't know if I'll be back again.

Written in Vleigenbos Campground, Amsterdam
by Marty J. Reeder 1999

To Friends on the road…

Paris

1. Paradise

It's hot and itchy on a tractor, in the middle of a hay field, in the Texas heat. I know because I grew up there. The dust from the hay rake will turn to mud behind the shirt collar and at the cuffs of long sleeves. There is the smell of diesel fuel, and on the hood, at the mouth of the fuel tank, there is a darkening ring like that behind the collar; and the sun is always baking.

It was comfortable inside my white truck, speeding along the dirt road to my home. The elm trees arched over the road before me with leaves covered in dust like snow. I saw the tractors working in the fields and pushed the gas pedal closer to the floor.

Home was a ranch twelve miles from the nearest paved road in Buffalo, Texas. My family raised cattle there. They also raised two boys, my older brother and me. He went to work for the coal-mine after high school and has been there ever since. I went away to expand my mind.

When I arrived at the ranch, my mother hugged me, then pointed out toward the field below our house to where my dad was working—a small ball of dust in the expanse of the country.

"Who's helping him?" I asked.

"No one."

"One man and two tractors," I looked at her lovingly.

"It takes a little longer, with you boys being gone." The twinkle in her eye said she understood, and she placed a gentle hand on my shoulder.

"I should go talk to him before I leave."

"Yes. You should."

I drove by the garden and across the tank dam. In the hay field, I turned off my engine and stepped out on to the brown grass. It was nice weather, and I watched the heat waves blur the image of his approach.

If it were any other day, I would have helped him finish the field. This was his paradise—the cattle, the land, the wide-open spaces. My paradise was out there, beyond the horizon, and this day, I was going to find it.

I was in love with a girl named Sarah, and she was in Paris, France. Three months earlier, a friend of mine had introduced me to her at a college party.

"Here's Sarah," he said, pushing her toward to me, "I'm going to find some dope."

She was beautiful, conversation was easy, and we spent our time talking about traveling Europe. She was going to study at the Sorbonne in Paris for the summer. I was going to travel Europe playing music for coins on the sidewalks. Of course, I was all talk until I met her.

Before she left, she held both of my hands, facing me, and said, "Marty, you *can't* not do this."

Her green eyes were full of adventure and in them I saw a world I had never seen—then she was gone.

The morning, before going to the ranch, I hocked everything that was mine and bought an open-ended ticket for France. I had earned my Bachelor's degree and quit my college job. For the first time in my life—I was free.

2. Pond Hopping

She wrote to me in her journal, never planning to send me a letter.

Sarah's journal

Hi, Marty. I went to see the Pere La Chaise cemetery today. It was simply overwhelming. Once I got in, I couldn't find my way out. So I just wandered around There for about an hour. I saw Jim Morrison's grave. I really don't see what the big deal is about it.
I've spent this whole day alone; I just feel like being alone today for some reason. I went to the cemetery alone and braved the metro alone and feel pretty good.
I am really excited about your coming here. In a way, though, I am dreading it because once you are here, we will have just a few days together, and then, once you leave, I will be so confused. I don't know what is going to happen next. Ever since the beginning of our relationship we said that we would meet in Paris, and then you would go

on your travels. Now that the time is almost here, I am scared that Paris might be the last time I ever see you. I know that I shouldn't waste my time worrying about things that I can't do anything about. It's just that when it comes to you, it's hard to live by the "whatever happens…happens" philosophy. I wish I had more control over the situation, but I don't. When the situation involves your heart, there is no way of controlling it no matter how much you might want to.

I sound really silly, don't I? You see, that's what spending the whole day alone will do to someone.

I'm supposed to be going to dinner with Lisa and Brent in about thirty minutes. We are going to Planet Hollywood. Only because it is the Fourth of July and we want to be American for a night.

July 4, 1999, Paris

When the stewardess offered me something to drink, I asked for a beer. When I found out that drinks were included with the price of the ticket, I had a few more. It was a red-eye flight and there was room on the plane to stretch out. The sky was dark outside my window and cool air hissed from the vent above me. I turned off the light and fell into sleep.

The following is a list of things in my pack, tucked into the overhead compartment along with my guitar zipped inside a gig bag:

Cargo pants	Two pair (one on, the others packed)
Shirts	Three (one on, the other two packed)
Underwear and socks	Three of each (one set on, the others packed)
Insulated rain coat	One (I kept it rolled and tied on the side of my pack, but I lost it in Amsterdam--damn)
Biker tent	One (yellow, the size of a coffee can, when packed, and tied to other side of pack)
Knives	Two (small one for food, etc., large one for protection. In 1999, you could board a plane with such items in your carry-on.)
Thick blanket	One (I used this for a bedroll; later it doubled for a poncho when I lost my coat and cut a hole in the middle of it to slip over my head and around my neck.)
Map	One (from a world highway atlas. I tore just the European section.)
Compass	One (I never used it, and left it with the Aussies in Belgium.)

Camera	One (with two rolls of film. With 48 shots I would take pictures of only the things that mattered.)
Journal	I had a fresh journal with Sarah's address in Paris written on the cover and three pens for writing.

In my pocket, I had my passport, one thousand five hundred dollars—and dreams of adventure.

Sarah's Journal

Okay, this really sucks. You called twice but I was never able to catch the call. I got your messages, but I don't know how to reach you. I don't even know when you are leaving for Amsterdam. I don't know anything. I was stressed out about it at first because I have no idea when you were leaving, when you were planning on being in Paris, etc…, but, now I don't care. If you come here, I will be very excited, and if you don't, I will be very sad, but I am not going to stress out about it anymore. I will just see you when I see you. I hope that I get to see you soon because if you take too long I might have a French boyfriend! Just kidding.

They do have an odor like no other, that's for sure. There's nothing like the strong smell of body odor to drive a person wild, eh? Did you ever notice that Body odor smells a lot like onions? Why is that?

I should probably go to bed now, but I can't sleep. I really wish that I could...never mind. It is pointless to wish for such things right now. Good night.

Paris, July 8, 1999

The last we spoke, my plans were to go to Amsterdam first, buy a Euro Rail Pass, and travel to Paris. Instead, I flew straight to Paris. It is just how it happened.

With my pack and guitar on my back, I walked off the plane at Charles DeGaulle airport.

Being from Texas, I speak almost fluent Spanish and not a bit of French. Out of fear and excitement I put one foot in front of the other and followed the crowd.

At the money exchange, I turned fifty dollars into francs then followed the signs to the metro (subway). I had no idea where I was going, or if I had paid too much for the ticket.

3. Good Luck

The rhythm of the rail was a nice change from the humming of the plane. The windows were down, and the air was thick and humid. The sky was bright and clear and I thought of Sarah being somewhere out there—a needle in the haystack that was Paris.

The day was young, too young to head straight for Sarah's dorm. I knew from phone conversations that she usually ate lunch in Luxemburg Park. When I overheard a young couple speaking English I asked them how to get there. The young lady pointed to the map printed above the door.

"Hey, where are ya'll from?" I almost shouted.

"England," the young man said while turning to face me.

"Here on holiday," she finished.

I moved my gear to the seats across from them. They had never been to America but knew a lot about Texas; I could tell by the questions about tumbleweeds, outhouses and shootouts. I told them about Sarah and how I planned to find her eating lunch in Luxembourg Park.

"Good luck," the young lady said exiting the

train; the young man waved and I watched them disappear, my first friends on the road.

Three stops later the train slowed to a stop at the Luxembourg station. The doors opened, and off I went, up the stairs and into the city — into the world outside of paradise.

4. Needle In The Hay

A little red car with blaring horn scurried through the crowded traffic. Across the road and to the left a McDonalds served fast food. Everyone seemed to be in a great hurry. I stood watching for a moment. It was a busy city, and now I was glad I had decided to wear my cap instead of my cowboy hat.

Behind me were the gates to Luxemburg Park. I passed the ice cream lady and the air was cool on the shaded path that led into the wonderland. Pea-gravel crunched beneath my feet and my stomach was growling.

I saw every face in every crowd, and searched every shaded bench, but didn't see her. There was a symphony playing Mozart in a gazebo near the center of the park. The music filled my soul and made everything even more surreal. Hours before I was on a dirt road in Texas.

Then I heard her calling. It was like waking from a deep sleep and her voice was my gentle alarm. I turned to see her coming towards me, waving and walking over like I had seen her yesterday.

Her green eyes were my destiny. My arms rose away from me reaching out to her.

My Journal

> June 9, 1999. Holy shit, I'm here; what an adventure so far, I did it, I found my way to Luxemburg Park on the train system, I don't know how but I did, it was crazy, and what do you know, I'm walking halfway through and I hear the sweetest voice in a heavy Texas accent say, "HEY."
> It was all she had to say and I knew it was her; she has never been so beautiful.
> She told me where I could buy a cheap sandwich and she went to class. I ate my first "French" meal: ham-and- cheese with tomatoes on a baguette! Damn, it was good—either that or I was starving and now I'm not.
> She will be back in about fifteen minutes and we are going to spend the weekend together. Right now I'm just sitting here at some age old Parthenon, chillin' in the shade, tourists everywhere. I found her…hey, I can see the Eiffel tower!

We spent that evening around St. Michelle. We bought wine at the market and had beer with our dinner outside a small café. Notre Dame Cathedral, across the river, sat beautiful and majestic, purple in the setting sun.

The weekend blew by us. It wasn't until Monday morning, when she returned to class, that I was alone again.

My Journal

June 11. I just got out of the shower. The last two days have been a breeze; I've spent every moment with my sweetie. It has been great.

Our first night here we bought two big — really big — 1664 beers and drank them with our dinner. Dinner was great, beer was great; and then we took bottles of wine and walked along the river bank. We stopped at some steps that went down to the water and drank a bottle. That was the best time I'd ever spent with her, romantic, we were in Paris and drinking wine together, watching the hordes of tourists going by on boats. Passionate kisses. People took pictures of us from the boat and I wish I had one, but for me that's a moment that can never be captured except in the realms of my mind.

After that bottle we began walking in the direction of the Eiffel Tower, the sun was getting low on the horizon. Halfway there we were halfway through our second bottle. We carved our initials next to many others on a tree. Some of the names were old; ours were fresh and new.

We were drunk when we finally arrived at the Tower. The lights were bright and hazy, and we danced to music no one else could hear until we fell from being dizzy, and then sat laughing on a bench. The lights of the tower were hazy above us.

5. E Music

Non-students were not allowed in the American coed dormitory. Knowing the code to the front door helped me blend in. Her room was on the fourth floor, first door on the left.

Beyond her door I was safe, and it became my Paris home. The floor was cool cement with pits and cracks, and it was browned with age. There were cracks in the plaster on the walls, and peeling paint. With no air conditioning the large arched windows were always opened and calling for a breeze from the courtyard below.

She had an ashtray on her wooden desk next to a lamp and a pack of Dunhill cigarettes. Her bed had a metal frame and was horrible for comfort. I spent every night on the floor, and every morning watching her dress by the mirror near the window.

One day, while losing myself in the city, I met the most extraordinary person. Sarah was in class and I wandered down to this place on the river called the island. It was near St. Michelle.

I saw a black man sitting in the shade along the cobblestone bank. The guitar he played looked as road worn as he did. His bare feet dangled over the bank. Beside him was an opened can of fruit, a half eaten chicken leg, and a tattered plastic bag. He was wearing a black top-hat.

I sat down beside him and opened up my case then offered him some wine from the bottle I was drinking. He accepted by pouring into his mouth never touching the bottle to his lips. Then he stood up and poured some over his feet, saying something in a language I had never before heard.

His name was E. He had songbooks in the tattered plastic sack. As he passed them over to me he spoke in broken English.

"I want to hear America."

I looked through them, smiling. I knew many of the songs by heart. I passed the Hendrix book back to him, opened to the page where the music and lyrics to *RED HOUSE* were printed. Then I poured my soul into the song and let the music take me over.

When I looked up he was happy. The yellow whites of his eyes were big and watery. He slapped my back and shook my hand, unable to speak.

E, who I later learned was an African refugee, had never heard the Blues.

My Journal

> I don't know what it is about the island on the river. It's the end. Today I was there and met a fellow from Africa. He offered me some smoke, but I passed and we began to play. Interesting character: fried chicken, can o' fruit, joint, top hat, bag of songs and one beat-to-hell, well-played, old-ass, Gib-

son guitar. It's funny we were in tune with each other. I learned a lot, and so did he.

When I was about to leave, he began to speak of people and who everybody was and how he could not understand why race always had to be an issue. In his country it's the Brits against the Africans. In my country it's the Anglos. He was glad that we were past that and he wished everyone could be. In music there is no race; together we shared and learned, and that, we really liked. I'm glad I met him and hope to see him again soon. I think of my day's adventures while she studies, my love.

6. A Girl Like Me

I waited for her on the steps leading down to our spot along the Seine River. I saw her walking across the bridge. I watched her like a day dream, approaching through the crowd.

She had her guitar slung of over her shoulder like I had mine. She was wearing a little sundress and smiling only at me. I was the luckiest man in the world, and college and Texas seemed like a lifetime away.

"I have on nothing beneath this dress," she said hugging me and kissing my cheek.

She smelt nice and the thin fabric felt like nothing. She flashed a playful look and trotted away, down to the river.

My Journal

Last night was beautiful; there are no other words to describe the way I felt. I fell in love, and I cried. I know now that I can never go on without her. She is like a dream. Am I dreaming? Nothing has ever been so perfect. I have never felt the way I did last night looking at her, and I know I never will again for another. I cried Tears of I-don't-know-what; I wasn't sad. I had just never before experienced the beauty of true love. The two of us, alone on the bank, made the most beautiful music. I have never played so well; it was as if we were making love through our guitars. I will never forget that night.

A guy came out of the dark behind us and knelt beside us and sang, "I met a girl like me." He took a sip of wine and disappeared. He sang like Jim Morrison.

What's with this city? There is a force I had never felt before.

I told her she was great at playing the guitar. Her response, "you taught me everything I know" is what made me cry. She wore my necklace and a dress, nothing more. She is cool beauty like I've never found before. My heart burns for her; she is the girl of my dreams.

I knew that I had found my true love. It was a wonderful and horrible feeling. I loved her and wanted to be near her, but there were many miles un-traveled calling my name.

7. Distance

My Journal

July 15. This morning I left her. I already miss her, but it is good for both of us to be apart. Only time will tell if the love we share for each other holds true. She is my angel in my heaven of freedom; I long to see her again. Until then my love…

I am now on my way to Amsterdam. I have three hundred dollars and I don't know how to get back. The view of countryside from the train is awesome. There are WWI or WWII graveyards everywhere and small stone houses. It's just like "The Dirty Dozen". It's beautiful and very moving. I like that; once again I am on the move…

The bullet train slowed to a stop in Amster-dam's Central Station. I stepped out on to the depot with my bag and guitar. My love was in Paris. My spirit was again racing for the horizon.
Outside of Central Station is the crisp moist air

that is Amsterdam. Tall skinny buildings line the canals, side by side, with hoist joints above the attics. Yellow trams go gliding by, drivers waving and ringing bells. Bicycle highways lead into the city, a million bicycles parked in front of Central Station alone. Like Lewis and Clark I stood on the edge of discovery.

"Clear the bike path, sir!" Someone spoke, pedaling by and ringing a bell.

I stepped up on the curb and walked into the city.

Sarah's Journal

Marty,
You left earlier today. At first I must admit that I was a little relieved to be on my own again, but now I am sad that I can't see you. I went straight to the metro after phonetics class instead of meeting you on the steps of the Parthenon. I knew then that I am going to miss you a lot. Now that my day is over, I am the saddest. I had so much fun spending this time with you. I really don't know how to put it into words, so maybe I shouldn't even try. I just know that I am sitting in a garden by my dorm; thinking of you and wishing so much that you were here it hurts.
Sarah, Paris July 1999

My
Amsterdam

8. Vliegenbos

In Amsterdam, it is legal to buy and smoke marijuana, and you can carry small quantities of it around in your pocket. Marijuana is sold at establishments called "coffee shops," where menus advertise different buds for sale. The buds are kept in plastic containers behind the counter and the proprietor will let you smell samples. Most coffee shops also provide smoking devices such as pipes, bongs, hookahs, rolling papers, lighters, and ashtrays, to be used inside the establishment. This is all legal.

After my first thirty minutes in the city, I was higher than I had ever been in my life. It was scary and fun at the same time, and that's the best way for me to describe my Amsterdam—scary and fun, in a beautiful city.

I was walking around, admiring the architecture and canals, with two buds of Orange Skunk in a small plastic bag and some rolling papers in my pocket. My mind was foggy, but my thoughts were clear. I asked a policeman for directions to the campground where I planned to make my home.

I showed him the piece of paper I carried in my

wallet. It had "Vliegenbos" written on it. Vliegen-bos, a place I had found on the internet back in Texas, was a campground outside the city. It was a place where I could stay for around fifty bucks a week. The policeman told me where to wait for the bus that would take me there.

I waited for the bus on a bridge where a soft breeze rippled the canal below. I was kneeling, resting my legs, like my dad often did after a long days work in the hayfield. For a moment I felt his genes inside of me, and I thought about him; how, in all of his life, he had never been more than sixty miles away from home. Then I began giggling, for no reason, and I had to walk away until I could contain myself.

9. Texas

"Ha-llo." The check-in girl had green eyes and a friendly smile behind the Vliegenbos counter.

"I need space to stay for a week."

"Okay and where are you from?"

Her accent would set any man's hormones into a radical frenzy and I was not immune. She had brunette, braided pig tails that hung down to her chest. She was beautiful, much larger than me with perfect proportions.

"Texas." I said.

"How long you stay?" She had rhythm to her syllables and her eyes were sparkling.

"One week."

"Okay, Texas, here is your tent number. Make sure it is attached to your tent at all times. Please pay the fee."

"Yes, ma'am." In a daze, I fumbled through my money and paid her the equivalent of fifty American dollars.

She never stopped smiling at me.

Walking through the campground was like the first day of being a new kid at school. I heard German, French, Swiss, Spanish, Italian and other languages I did not know. Tents were everywhere. I could have never imagined so many tents so close together.

Trying to act like I had it all together, I chose a small spot next to the back fence to stake my claim. There was a guy that looked my age packing up his camp—moving out.

"Hey." He was smoking a joint. "Where you from?" He asked.

"Texas."

"No shit." He walked over to me, smiling, and reached out to shake my hand. "I'm from Austin."

"I'll be damned." I shook his hand and took the joint he passed me. He was one of those cool guys—blonde hair, no shirt, sexy girlfriend, didn't seem to have a care in the world.

He was leaving to catch a plane back home, and we only talked while he was packing.

"Say hello to Texas," I said as he walked away. He just waved and never looked back.

So, I took over the land that was already known for Texas. And later, when the gypsies learned where I came from, that became my name. Texas.

10. Dublin

The green eyed one, with the red hair and freckles, had Ireland written all over her. They were walking through the tents toward me. It was raining. Her friends didn't look Irish at all.

They didn't seem worried about being wet and I was putting on my new rain coat. The man of the group, Grant, introduced the girls first and then himself. He was dark skinned like me and had thick curly hair. Maread was the red haired one, and Charlie was short for Claire.

They had the two tents in front of mine. Charlie and Maread shared one, Grant had the other. We arranged them so the three doors faced each other and we had our own little courtyard. While doing so, the rain stopped and we all put on dry clothes to fight the chill.

As I got to know my Irish friends, days went by in Amsterdam. I learned about life in Dublin, and picked up their accent hanging around with them.

When school was out, Dublin was a boring place to be. Everyone left for the summer, to stay there was a tortuous bore. Grant, Maread, and Charlie traveled to Spain, then to Morocco. They were separated in Paris and met up in Amsterdam. All of them were nearly out of money and looking for work.

Grant later found work in a café washing dishes—anything to keep from returning home before school started. Maread had an aunt in England who owned a pub. She and Charlie would eventually take a train there to work and live in a small apartment above the bar.

I told them about Sarah.

We all had our own agendas, but we stuck together for a while in Amsterdam.

11. Days

The Irish showed me how to get to the city without riding the bus, and I never rode the bus again. The path from Vliegenbos to the Het IJ takes fifteen minutes. The walking is flat and easy and there is a supermarket halfway through the suburbs.

(The Het IJ is the bay connecting Amsterdam to the North Sea. It is busy with large ships and barges and an industrial landscape. There is a free ferry for pedestrian and bike traffic only. It runs across the bay to the rear of Central Station from early morning to late at night.)

The Irish and I would leave camp together every morning, leaving our gear zipped inside our tents. Grant had found a place with the cheapest coffee and breakfast, and we often ate outside, beside the canal in front of the small cafe. From there we went on our own for the day.

I would lose myself in the city, walking along the narrow streets along the canals, playing my guitar for coins in Dam Square, and relaxing in Vondel Park. A daily tour of the Heineken factory was great for a cheap buzz.

One day, when I had done exceptionally well

playing music in the city, I sprung for a case of beer. Grant and I split the load to the campground. That night, I wasn't surprised when little Maread drank me under the table in true Irish fashion.

Fires were not allowed in Vliegenbos. It was nice to have the candles gathered from town lit all at once and placed in the middle of our little court-yard. We often had visitors: Dave, from California; Vale, the Scottish gypsy; and Nadia, from Switzer-land, who spoke five different languages and often farted when she was drinking and laughing.

I learned a lot about the world in those late night gatherings—listening to stories from distant lands that were now closer to me than my home; and there was always me with my guitar, and the music, keep-ing Sarah close to me, in my heart.

Sarah's Journal

> Marty,
> Friday and Saturday were Crazy!!! I am in the park where I found you. Some man came and kissed me on the mouth, so I guess I have kissed a Frenchman. It really freaked me out. He just came and talked to me, and when he got up to leave, he gave me two pecks on the mouth! The French are so weird.
> I have actually kissed four Frenchmen since you left. I haven't decided if I am going to tell you that yet or not. I have been out club-bing with Heather two nights in a row. Both nights we didn't return until after 6 am.

Three out of the four kisses were not exactly voluntary though, in my defense. One guy shoved his tongue down my throat while we were dancing, and my friend Linda slapped him. It was pretty cool. She is from New York, and she knows how to deal with freaks and assholes better than I do, being such a friendly Texan.

One guy, the one I voluntarily allowed to kiss me, was Phillipe. He was very nice. He called me yesterday to ask me to go with him to a barbecue, but I didn't. I think I might see him again though. I can use him to practice my French because his English is not so good. He is okay, but he just makes me miss you so much more.

Oh Marty, I want to see you so bad I can't think of anything else. Your face is everyplace I go. I don't know if I can last two weeks until I see you again. I feel so cut off from you. I can't even call you.

You called this morning and I missed your call by a couple of seconds and just lay in my bed for an hour staring at the wall. I have never felt so frustrated. I have all of these men all over me, and all I want is you!

I wish you could be here to protect me from them. I don't want to kiss any more French boys, damn it! I know that you want me to be free, but I just want to be with you. I don't want to be set free like that; At least I don't think I do.

Sarah, Paris July 18, 1999

[37]

12. Thieves

My Journal

Last night I became one of them—of the culture I moved into. It's as if we are all aliens living in a world of confusion. I have never been away from home this long, or this far away. I feel the change in me has really started; this is where I break down. To build a man, you must first break him.

Last night I realized just how far away home really is. I am on the world. Texas is somewhere these people have never been. I am the TEXAN. That's what my friends—the Irish, the Scots, and the Swiss—call me. We are all travelers, and we are many. Today I had to get away. They are my friends, but I need my solitude. I am lost, on the verge of crying at every thought of home and the people I left behind.

I am on the world, on my adventure, a long journey with a long way to go. It is beautiful here, but I'm ready to leave. I wish so much to return to my love in Paris, to be in the shelter of her loving arms, but I can't. I must stick it out alone. I can hold only her memory close to me.

I call, but when I do I cannot speak. I'm losing control of my emotions. If I would let them, tears would follow my every thought of her, or of home, but I won't let them. I fight them back and enjoy the day and my time here. These "times" I will never live again.

You have to be careful here; you have to watch your belongings as well as your mind, or you can lose them.

While writing that, I was sitting on some steps in Dam Square. I had smoked my mind the night before. I lit a rolly and watched the homeless teens playing in the square. I worried for their futures. One of them stole my raincoat while I was lost in thought. Damned Square.

Sarah's Journal

I sent my postcards off today. I have been carrying them around with me for two weeks, so it's about time. Phillipe called me this morning at 7:30! I answered the phone, and once I realized that it was him, I hung up on him. I doubt that he will call back. I don't really know why I did that. It was just my first instinct, so I went through with it. Au revoir, Phillipe!

I am drinking some really bad wine right

now. It is from Spain. It's gross. I cooked myself dinner tonight. I made vegetable couscous; it wasn't bad. I am starting to get tired already. I guess I still haven't recuperated from this weekend. I'm starting to doubt I will ever let you read this. Maybe you shouldn't know everything that I have written; I'm not really sure. I will continue to write, though, about my experiences here. Even if you never read this, I know that I will one day, and I won't be able to read a single page without thinking of you.

Oh, shit!

Phillipe just called.

He is coming to visit me…what do I do? Why am I doing this? Maybe I am doing it for you in some way. You said that you want me to be free. Maybe I am just trying not to disappoint you. Oh, shit. I don't know. I'm so confused.

Sarah, Paris July 19, 1999

13. Phillipe

So, Phillipe came to visit me last night. He brought us a really good bottle of wine, a bottle of Malibu Rum and some orange juice. He also brought some Hashish. He stayed until about 3:30 this morning. He helped me with my homework, and we talked to each other in French most of the time. I thought that was pretty cool.

I told myself that I wasn't going to, but I ended up kissing him at the end of the night. I don't know why; I wasn't even drunk this time. He was a lot more attractive than I remember. He said that he was going to call me today, but I don't think that I will answer the phone. It's time for me to end this before I do something that I regret. I already regret my behavior; I can't let it get any worse.

You called this morning. It seemed weird. So much has happened since you left. I only hope that you won't notice a change in me. It will be weird for me to act as though nothing has happened. I'm sure that, after a day or two, the truth will come out. Then we will know where we stand. I think, in a way, it will be good for us.

But, then maybe that's just bullshit.

Maybe I just fucked everything up.

Was this a test?

Did I pass or fail?

I'm sure that I have failed, and that is why you can never read this. Oh Marty, if you only knew how much I miss you and really want to be with you and only you, if you knew that, you wouldn't care about what has happened here in the past few days.

Sarah, Paris July 20, 1999

14. Gypsy

My Journal

> Today is cool. I sit stoned on a bench with my Irish friends; the girls leave today, off to London to work in Auntie's pub. Grant is staying, he's found work and will be at the campsite for another week. I plan to start my journey to Paris on Thursday. I still don't know how. I'm not scared of walking.
> Today, however, I spend with my friends on their last day here. I love them like family. I will miss them. Friends on the road…

The city of Amsterdam furnishes bicycles to the public. The bikes are not well taken care of and have no locks. To properly use the bike, you must ride it and leave it at your destination. If it is not there when you come back, then someone else must have needed it. Grant rode one into Vliegenbos one evening after the girls had left.

We were surprised to find it there in the morning. Someone did take the seat, which made Grant not want to ride it. He left it. I took it, and he flipped me the bird as I passed him on the way out of the park.

With the bike, I did not take the ferry. I followed the route I first took by bus. I rode through neighborhoods of colorful houses and well-kept yards. Not many people owned cars.

In the city, I parked in front of a little music store where I spent hours playing fine Spanish guitars and stand-up bases. When I came out, the bike was as I had left it. Having no seat was an advantage.

I remember riding beside a large Dutchman in a business suit. He was riding an expensive bike and made me feel pretty small the way he looked down on me. I felt like a vagabond, I looked like a vagabond, but damn it, I was a gypsy.

Someone took my bike soon afterward.

15. Australia

My Journal

> WOW, Amsterdam is cool. I must move on though; I'm beginning to feel at home away from home, one thing, traveling is definitely an adventure; for one to know this, one must experience life after the sickness, the sickness of life away from home, life on the road. Cheers…

Drops of water splashed from the waves below the ferry. The sun had started its decent on the horizon. I had no money for the train to Paris.

I knew they were looking for Vliegenbos. They were wearing packs and one of them had a guitar slung over his shoulder like me. I introduced myself and they put their map away.

The two guys were fair skinned and wore long hair. The two ladies, a blonde and brunette, were beautiful.

With the Irish disbanded, the Aussies became my new family.

James-n-Bee and Mic-n-Meg were from Melbourne, Australia. Mic's family had a cattle ranch in Tasmania where all of them spent lots of time. They were a lot like me, and I spent most of the remainder of my time in Amsterdam with them.

I Come from the Land Down Under was our song of choice most nights. James often played a didgeridoo that also functioned as their fishing pole case.

I soon learned that James and Mic knew a lot about fish. They went to school together in Melbourne and worked together with the Aboriginees. Their science was that of genetic fish breeding and fish crop cultivation.

Bee called them "fish fuckers."

She and Meg also worked with the Aboriginal people.

As I got to know them, I felt like the time I had spent with Sarah had long since passed. I was different now, just as I had become different when I stepped off the plane in Paris. I missed her. I had to get back to Paris before she forgot who I was.

16. My Right Of Passage

"These stones represent the edges of the world," Mic told me one night in their small cabin in the campground. We gathered around the little table built into the wall. It was dark out and the moon was full.

The brittle paper James was unfolding had a cross drawn in charcoal and was marked with N, S, E, W. He placed small polished stones at each corner holding the paper flat beneath the flickering shadow. He shot me a serious look with a little smile.

"This is an Aboriginal travel ritual, Ma-tee. Since we're all travelers on the land, it is customary to perform this ritual to see if we should go on from here together."

"The Aborigines do this when they are traveling and become friends with strangers," Meg added, smiling.

James emptied half of a small pouch of pebbles into my hand. The other half he poured into his hand. He said something in Aboriginal tongue that sounded dark and mystical. Then, he threw the pebbles onto the paper. Most of them fell on the lower right quadrant.

"Southeast, now you," he moved so I could reach the table.

With a little coaching, I repeated the words and threw my pebbles.

"Southeast," Mic said, slapping my back. "Looks like you're going with us, mate!"

Sarah's Journal

I missed your call today. You said you would call in the morning, though. I hope you find your way to Switzerland with your Australian friends. Maybe it's better for us to be apart another week. So much has happened to me in just one week, I know that more is sure to happen in the next. A really big part of me just wants you to come back to Paris. I miss your face and your laugh and the laid back times we have spent together. I like being with you. You are so easy to be with. I don't have to try and act any sort of way; I can just be myself and know that you like me.

Another WEEK! I'm scared to think of what's to come. It's already going to be weird when I see you again, but if I have to double the timeframe, is it going to be doubly weird? Everything happens for a reason, right? Maybe the next week will show me whatever it is that I need to see. I know that this has been the week of confusion; maybe next week will be one of revelation. If you were here you might cloud up whatever it is that I need to see or discover. So my rational side says, "go to Switzerland, and I will meet you in a week." My irrational heart says, "Come back to Paris!" Oh, which to listen to? I don't know.

Sarah, Paris

On another night in Amsterdam, I was given my Aboriginal spirit name. The girls asked me a series of questions about myself and my perceptions, scoring each answer with a number between one and ten.

"White Wolf," Bee said after the tally.

"White Wolf," I repeated, smiling.

The girls may have been pulling my leg, the guys were shaking their heads and smirking behind them during my inquisition, but I liked it, and I kept the name.

The
Open Road

17. SUMMER OF 1969

My Journal

> I'm sitting in an Irish pub in Amsterdam
> with the Aussies, drinking a beer and smok-
> ing a joint I just rolled. This is my last day in
> Amsterdam, with good friends, good people.
> I think of home, where I've been, and where
> I'll go. Today I go toward Paris with my
> friends, my new family of Australians, good
> people with whom I feel at peace. We travel
> by van (kombi) southeast, as the rocks fell.
> White wolf is no longer astray.

The Aussies bought a green joker Volkswagen
van from a man in Amsterdam. It was straight out
of the sixties, with the pop up camper and a kitch-
enette. I took a picture of them all standing in front
of it. Soon, we were traveling across Holland, passing windmills and fields of sunflowers, listening to
a Jimi Hendrix mix tape that Mic had brought
along.

In Australia, transportation, such as the van, is
called a "Kombi." So, I understood that "Kombi"
was slang for jalopy.

They also drive on the wrong side of the road.

"Who says it's wrong?" James shouted, almost
sideswiping a pedestrian.

"Opposite," Mic added above the cursing. "We

drive on the opposite side of the road. You drive on the wrong side of the road."

I held on. We almost sideswiped everything and yielding was just dangerous.

"No worries, mate."

Sarah's Journal

Yesterday we had a barbeque downstairs in the basement. We had tons of food: hamburgers, fruit, chocolate cake, etc...it was okay. After that a bunch of us went to Tammie's room and drank and played cards. We just about finished off the Malibu rum that Philippe brought me. I passed my guitar around and people played it. After that, Uman, Sainjeve, Angela, Lisa, Brent, and I went to a bar called Chez Georges. It was very cool. You walk downstairs into this underground tunnel-looking cave thing that is illuminated only by candles. The music was great. It was oldies, jazz, Indian and Egyptian or something. It is a place that has obviously been tucked away since the sixties and far out of the tourist's eye. Angela got sick. We went to get coffee while the others were still inside. She puked on the curb while some stupid French boys cheered her on. The waiter gave us coffee for free. I doubt that happens very often in Paris. Anyway, we got home at about 1:30am. Not too late, but I still felt like an ass this morning. You called to tell me that you were leaving

Amsterdam in a van with Australian friends. I guess that you may be here Sunday or Monday, that they may drop you in Luxemburg and you can catch a train to Paris. Wow, this is going to be weird. You are coming all this way to see me and what if things aren't how you expect them to be? What if things have changed between us already? There is no way of knowing until you get here. I wish you could just go to Switzerland with your friends; that way it won't cost you anything extra to find out that I am now an even bigger freak than before. I don't know how to tell you not to come. How can I do that?

Sarah, Paris July 23, 1999

18. Riding In A Burned Out Kombi

In Australia, vegemite is the equivalent of peanut butter. It's dark and thick like tar. Mothers feed it to their children and their children grow up and feed it to Texans they meet in Amsterdam.

We were all eating vegemite sandwiches in an RV park north of Haarlem on in the Duinterrein Velsen. Part of Hitler's Atlantik Wall stood well preserved hidden in the dunes on the bay.

Not knowing the laws about marijuana outside of Amsterdam, we decided it would be best to smoke the rest of our stash there—in the gun turret of one those massive bunkers over looking the beach.

Afterward, James and Bee went to explore the other bunkers. Mic and Meg went for a walk along the shore. I was sitting on a sand dune alone.

My Journal

Sarah, I wish you were here; it is beautiful. The wind is cold and at my face. It would be fun to feel the warmth of your touch, to feel your love. First day on the road... life is good. WWII bunkers, sand dunes, ocean, food, friends, the love of Sarah: I AM ALIVE! This is life beyond my life so far; I've seen things I have never seen or thought I would...life on the road.

These bunkers are massive, a whole row of them connected by underground tunnels, providing total harbor defense, a great place for shelter from the storm of the future from our past.

The Aussies were learning how to drive and I was sitting in the back with the girls, thinking about Sarah. We were traveling east from Haarlem, then south along the western edge of Germany. There was a pit of sorrow in my stomach like in the fourth grade when I was dumped by Gina Rushing. Yet, the call of freedom had my number and I rode in peace not knowing what adventures were ahead.

That night, Mic and I were knee deep in a river playing music like we had never played before.

19. I Hate Bunny Rabbits

The kombi broke down at a campground near La Roche-en-Ardenne, a small town in the upper Belgian Ardennes. It was our third day on the road. I paid for a spot of my own and set up my tent on the bank of the river.

For days to come we would work on the van by day and sit around my fire at night. It was one of those nights that I learned to hate bunny rabbits.

Meg said it first, pointing her pinky finger at the smoke from the campfire. Her brunette hair and dark eyes were shimmering in the fire light, and the smoke went away from her.

A little later, I saw Bee do the same thing. Mic and James saw me notice this, and I could tell they were waiting for me to ask what the hell was going on. So, I did.

"I hate bunny rabbits," Bee said and pointed her finger at the fire again. "It keeps the smoke away."

"What?"

"When the smoke comes in your face, point your finger at it and say, I hate bunny rabbits, and the smoke will go away." Meg said.

I could never tell if these two were pulling my leg, but I tried it, and the smoke went away.

When they returned to the camper, I was alone. There were the sounds of the river, and I had no way of contacting Sarah.

Sarah's Journal

I had to get up today at 6 am to catch our bus to Loire Valley. We rode for about two hours. I slept and listened to music on my headphones.

The chateau was nice. We ate by the river and then went to another chateau; that was boring. Then we went to a wine tasting place, and I bought two jars of champagne jelly. That was pretty fun. Then we went out to eat at this really nice restaurant. We ate a four-course meal. I feel as big as a house. You probably won't even find me attractive anymore because I've gained so much weight!! Tomorrow we are going to see two more chateaus and another wine place. I'm tired; I'd rather just go back home.

I like riding on the bus. I got a lot of thinking done. I might actually see you tomorrow. I'm excited, but I know that I'm going to look like an ass—A fat ass too. I am going to be so busy tomorrow that I really kind of wish you wouldn't show up until Monday or Tuesday so I can do the things I need to do. I have a test on Monday and a paper due

Tuesday, and I have to spend time with mom now that she is here. Oh, well. I'm sure everything is okay. Goodnight.

Sarah, Paris July 24, 1999

20. Small World

Stuck in a valley by a river in the Ardenne Mountains was not a bad place to be. It was nice to have the "fish fuckers" with us. They both were great fisherman and we always had plenty to eat. I hiked for miles in those woods, barefooted on the pine needle carpet.

Our last night was spent with a large Belgian family on holiday: cousins, aunts, uncles, kids, beer, and food. We were all glad to accept the Belgian invitation—and did our best to entertain them in return.

Mic and James told stories about Australia and Tasmania around the bon fire and I told stories of Texas. One of the Belgian men knew every Hank Williams song ever written.

Another of the Belgians was a mechanic. He fixed the kombi the next day and, once again, we were on the road. The mechanic's wife, a beautiful black woman, was once from Texas, she told me. She came over one summer fifteen years ago and never returned.

Sarah's Journal

You weren't here when I got home and you

didn't call, so I have to assume that you aren't in Paris tonight. I have no idea when or even if to expect you, so that really sucks. Oh, well. I have a lot of shit to do tonight and tomorrow, so maybe it's good that you aren't here. I just have to keep telling myself that. Anyway, I guess I'd better shower and get to studying.

It's now 1:37 pm. I haven't studied or anything. I just took a shower, read my Judy Blume book, ate some peas and dried my hair.

I wish that you were here. I want a hug. I need a hug. I wish I knew what was going on. When will I see you again? Are you okay? I feel weird—like I will never see you again. Maybe you fell in love with some other girl. You did say that you fall in love easily. I must admit I don't find that comforting at all. I have only been in love once or maybe twice, now, but you never really know, do you?

Sarah, Paris July 25, 1999

In the town of Bastogne I told James to pull over. There were no Aboriginal travel rituals for parting ways and it was time. They were going to Germany. I was going to Paris.

I waved goodbye to them as they drove away, the girls at the back window like children, James' eyes in the rearview mirror, and Mic hanging out of the sliding door facing me until they were gone.

21. Freedom

"I go to Paris." I said aloud, walking across the road into the town.

There was no train station and no bus ride that followed a schedule. I borrowed a black marker from a shopkeeper and found a piece of cardboard. A curious lady watched me make a sign.

"The road you are looking for is over that mountain." She told me.

I looked to the right and saw the narrow road leading up the slope. This is what my cardboard sign read:

PARIS ☺

And then I was doing it. I was hitchhiking, just like I said I was going to do. It was like the deep end of the pool when you didn't know how to swim. You know it's dangerous, but you do it anyway because it seems fun and daring.

The pavement was wet and the greens of the trees were dark from the moisture in the night. "No worries, mate," I told myself, swallowing the huge lump in my throat that followed every thought of seeing the Kombi drive away.

Not far along, I passed an exploded Sherman tank. A plaque over looking the valley told the story of the Allied liberation of the area. I realized then that where I had been camping was not far from the Battle of the Bulge. I thought about that, and freedom, as I continued up the mountain road. My own bravery was nothing in comparison to the men who fought for freedom there.

22. Lifts

Not far past the war memorial my first lift arrived. The old man used the dirty little car as a crutch, walking around to open the trunk. The book I had read *(Rick Steve's The Back Door to Europe)* says, when hitching rides, never put your things in the trunk. Some people will let you out, and then speed off with your stuff before you can get it out. There was no room in the front of his little car, so I put my things in his trunk, and climbed in the passenger seat.

He spoke no English or Spanish, and smelt of old cheese. The ride was silent. I saw road signs that told me I was on the right path, and rode as far as he took me. I thanked him when he dropped me off.

"Merci, gracias, thank you, dank u wel."

It was fine weather and it's nice country there in Belgium, up in the hills, and after I walked for awhile I sat down and ate an apple. I looked out at the country and the valley down below. It was a beautiful day for freedom.

Thinking of Sarah, I continued on, there was a rhythm to my steps and I sang few songs to pass the miles. Two hours later, I was glad to see a little red car squeal to a stop in front of me. The windows were down. The music was blaring.

"You are lucky… I go to Paris." He smiled, turning down the volume and opening the door. He was a young chef with short, blonde hair. He was returning to Paris from a culinary school up north.

It was cool with the windows down, and the countryside, with its narrow roads passed me by.

23. The Border

"Do you have your passport?"

"Yeah," I said and turned around to retrieve my bag.

"Wait." He put his hand on my shoulder. "Wait."

The French border guard was looking inside the car with his mean, bulldog face. He motioned for us to pull over and get out.

"Don't worry." The chef was nervous parking the car.

Both of us were escorted from the car into a small brick building. On the way we passed another guard with a dog on a leash going toward the car.

I was locked in a windowless room where I spent an eternity thinking of the horrible things that were about to happen. When the guard returned, he threw my bag and guitar onto the large stainless steel table in the middle of the room. Two other guards stepped into the room and closed the door behind them.

In a thick accent, I was told to empty all of my gear. I went for my passport first. It was snatched and taken from the room. I continued unpacking and the two remaining guards searched everything.

One of them was reading my journal while the other opened the large knife I carried with me and inspected the blade. Unrolling my tent, they found some cigarette rolling papers and brought the dog in to sniff everything, including me.

"Damn, I lost my ride," I was thinking, with my hands on my head, smelling the brick wall, and a dog snout in my crotch.

The guard returned with my passport and threw it on the table. It slid across the stainless steel, hitting a small pile of coins and knocking them to the floor. He pointed at the guard nearest the door and motioned him outside. Ugly French words were exchanged between them, and then I was told to pack up and get out.

Back in the bright sunlight, I saw other cars being stopped. The guards waved me on. My ride was gone, and I walked back into France.

When rounding a corner two miles later, I saw the little red car parked up ahead. The chef was leaning on the trunk, lighting a cigarette.

Seeing me he waved with both of his hands and doubled over with laughter. "Get in," he said, stopping the car in reverse, and away we went, again flying down the road, listening to U2 and smoking cigarettes.

Like an old friend, he was making fun of me, holding up his hands with a dumb look on his face, like I had done at the border.

Soon, the city of Paris topped the horizon.

Bern

24. Foreign Land

Her arched shutters were opened high above me. Had it been a year since I had been there? For so long I had missed her and thought about her and now I stood beneath her window. For the first time I wondered—did she ever think of me?

Did she want me to come back? How long had I been gone?

"Sarah," I yelled cupping my hands over my mouth. I had to know. "Sarah,…she's not home," my happy heart fell to the pavement beside me.

Turning to walk away I saw her standing on the steps leading into the courtyard. I wondered how long she had been there looking at me. Her book bag was over one shoulder and she was wearing the sundress like before.

For a moment we stood looking, searching for a hint of the person we knew before.

When she smiled I melted, and then she was hugging me. I realized then that I had been gone a million years. I was madly in love with her and she was a stranger.

I spent that night on her floor staring up into darkness. I told her of my adventures. She told me of hers, and I kissed her, again and again—and wished the night to never end.

25. Paris

When I found E, he had a swollen eye and was carrying a club with his guitar case. Sarah was in class and I had spent the day playing music and taking coins from tourists. I never understood what happened to E. He told me about it, but I could not decipher his words. I did understand his warning to watch myself.

He was happy to see me and I felt right at home beside him on the island overlooking the Seine.

Sarah's Journal

You came in Monday night. You hitched from Belgium. You're crazy; do you know that?

I went to a play, Inesco, with mom last night. It was kind of funny and about how husbands and wives don't communicate with each other. After the play I had a beer with Mom and Wendy. Then you showed up (drunk and high from hanging out with your African friend on the river), and we went to the Greek restaurant for dinner. Food was bad; wine and entertainment were good. You bought mom and I each a rose.

Afterward, we said Goodbye to mom and Wendy and went to play and sing with the weird Algerians in front of Notre Dame. I got a beer while you, "The Texan," played. Oh, I forgot to mention that Monday night when we were sitting next to the river, a big boat went by and splashed nasty Seine water all over us!

Sarah, Paris July 29 1999

I washed my clothes in Sarah's sink and hung them by the window to dry. Three days had passed and I was getting around Paris like it was my own backyard. I was a street musician. I spoke English with a foreign accent. I was in love and I was a lover—and Paris was my home.

My funds were running low and playing music was more of a necessity than a pass-time. My Aussie buddies called Sarah's phone and left a message. They were on their way to Bern, Switzerland, and hoped I could meet them there.

Sarah's Journal

You are playing your guitar and sitting on the window sill. I need to pack for Switzerland, but I don't know what to take. I didn't go to my culture class today. I don't know why. I have been spending all my time with you since you arrived. I don't really mind even though I know that I should be mingling with others. Paris isn't for me. I'm glad that I found that out. I'm finding out so much here even though I know that this is not where I belong.

I Talked to Marty's old neighbor, Doc, today. He called all the way from sleepy hollow trailer park in Texas, just to check on Marty. I really like that old man; he is very sweet.

Most people I've met here speak three or four different languages. In America, we try so hard to be alike that we sacrifice the roots of our different cultures, and there you have it, the birth of racism.

Sarah, Paris July 30, 1999

26. The Elder

The older model passenger car wasn't crowded. Sarah was stretched out, her feet by the window, leaning into my arms. Outside was a world we had never before seen—mountains, forests, and lakes passing gently by. It was nice with her and the clacking motions of the rail.

Now that we were together, I never wanted us to be apart. But, like a dark cloud, there was the thought of losing her in trials of life still before us. How long could true happiness exist before it would become something taken granted?

Sarah's Journal

On the train to Switzerland. Marty went to the smoking car to smoke a rolly. The countryside is very beautiful. There are snow capped mountains and I saw cows with little bells around their necks, just like in the movies.

He came back and I just let him read some of my journal. Why do I feel so weird about that? I shouldn't want to keep secrets, but maybe there are just some things that one should keep to oneself. The longer you live, the more skeletons you have. Your past becomes part of you. It can be haunting, but sometimes telling secrets to the one you care about makes it not as frightening anymore. I love being honest because it keeps me sane, But maybe I am affecting the sanity of others while I am venting mine. Am I being selfish or Egotistical? I hope not. It is hard to know the minds of other people; you can't. Everyone thinks and reacts differently.

"Should we catch a tram?" Sarah asked me, looking at a map outside the station in Bern.

"Nahh, it's a beautiful day. We'll find it." We were looking for Eichholz, the campground where the Aussies were going to be.

Much of the city of Bern is from the medieval time period. The stone streets are narrow and not made for automobiles. We were walking with little direction in the breathtaking atmosphere around us.

We stopped in a small park near a fountain to rest. It was mid-afternoon and the air was cool. I kissed her there in the shade and we were happy to be out of Paris.

Along the way we were stopped by a little old man asking for the time. He spoke to me in Spanish and I noticed a pocket watch in his vest pocket.

He spoke of life and love and commented on Sarah's beauty being like the beautiful day. He was very kind and peaceful.

Leaving him, I noticed a certain sparkle in his eyes. It was as if they twinkled with the reminiscent thoughts of younger days.

He could have been me from the future, returning to the days he most loved.

27. Eichholz

My eyes were searching for the green kombi when we arrived at Eichholz. I was excited at the thought of seeing of my friends again.

Sarah, having more money than I did, paid for our stay for the weekend, and I bought some grilled bratwurst from the campground grill. It was the smell that led me to them. We ate by the river still shouldering our gear. Children were playing by the shore. Boats were floating by in the strong current and I was shocked by the coldness of the river when I dipped in to wash my hands.

The river current was fast and strong like our passion for each other—and dangerous.

Sarah's Journal

We're at the campsite in Switzerland. There are lots of Germans here; I've heard no English spoken. We are truly outsiders. We have kept to ourselves.

Last night we set up camp. After that we just hung out. Marty's tent is tiny. We slept in it last night; it was cool. This morning we went to the market and got sausage, bread, cheese, apples, oranges, beer and candles. We went for a hike and had a picnic on the river. We came back, and I lay in the sun and took a nap. Now I am off for the five minutes of hot water that I paid for!

Sarah, Bern, Switzerland, July 31, 1999

There was a sidewalk that ran along the bank of the river and we never saw the end of it. The river was fast and icy blue from the melting snow in Swiss mountains. It was the best water I ever tasted, and it was free.

Sarah and I were also free.

"This is living," I told her one morning. We were sitting on the mountainside overlooking a field of grain. We were eating apples and she was leaning against me.

28. Searching

On Saturday, I stood at the gates to the campground looking up the road. The Aussies weren't coming.

"No worries, mate," I told myself, kicking at the gravel, my hands in my pockets, like a disappointed child. Sarah had gone off alone. It was okay for us to do that—to want to be alone—right?

Sarah's Journal

> I am sitting under a tree by the water. Everyone is in bathing suits. I really wish that I had brought mine. Yesterday, when we went in the river, I had to wear boxers and a t-shirt. I felt really stupid. Marty left to go and look for his Aussie friends. I really hope that they come tonight. We have been hanging out with ourselves for a little too long. I don't like doing that. I am supposed to go and see him in Amsterdam this weekend, too. I really like him, but I've always hated spending too much time with one person, especially the one that you are trying to at-

tract because after awhile, you just can't be cute and appealing anymore. You just become a little too relaxed. You get that "been married for 15 years" attitude and you start burping and farting in front of each other. There is usually also a little too much whining on my part. So, I'm looking forward to going back to Paris and getting my shit back in order. My hands are sticky from my coke that spilled on me. I don't have much else to say. I'm kind of bored. I'm still searching for my place; it isn't here. I have 15,982 cities to go.

Sarah, Bern, Switzerland, August 1, 1999

My Journal

Here I find realization in peace. True studies, in the college of life, are now underway. Change flows fast, and I go with the wind, and with the wind goes my soul, life is ever changing, never to be understood.

Only at life's end will life ever be fulfilled, and lo' the day when you can look back and see what all you have done; realizing that materialistic items are of no value and that true richness is in the happiness and experience of life. Peace and love are the treasures of my life's journey, the knowledge of open-mindedness is the vessel in which I travel…life on the road, life within life, forever free, and peaceful.

The world before me, the past behind me

and the wind blows, I am free, and so is she,
my angel, Sarah.

Waiting for the train, I was smoking a rolly and
drinking a Cardinal (beer). Sarah was shopping in a
bookstore across the way. After my smoke, I played
a few songs and made a little coin.

She returned with a gift for me. It was a copy of
The Black Cat, a collection of short stories by Edgar
Allen Poe. I was reading *The Oblong Box* when the
train crossed over the French border.

My
Paradise

29. E

Walking around the narrow streets of St. Michelle, my mind was filled with thoughts of things I did not want to think about. There was an open ended ticket that would fly me away from there when ever I was ready. I was often hungry and it was easy for my spirit to darken—knowing that I could not go on like this forever.

Running from my fears I headed down the steps to the river, looking for my friend.

E had a new friend, Andreas, an acting student who was living across the river in a small apartment. He told Andreas that I was his brother and that I was like lighting and thunder. E was happy to see me, and I always felt happy with him there on the river.

Andreas sat and listened as we played. This time we did not play for tourists. We played for ourselves, for Africa and for Texas, for all of our joys and all of our sorrow, and when we were done I told E goodbye.

I thanked E for being my friend, and he was happy to let me take a picture of him. He had Andreas get in the shot with him; so that when I got back home I would see him with company and re-member him as never being alone.

"Be careful, my brother," he said hugging my neck. He stank, as usual, but I didn't care. I hugged him back and walked away.

He yelled to me Swahili tongue as I was going up the steps and away from the river. I turned around to see him on the island with his arms spread wide, one hand was pointing toward the sky. He held the guitar out toward me with the other. The Eiffel tower was jutting out of the horizon behind him, and I stood there watching his splendorous dance. He was a happy spirit and I knew it would be the last I ever saw of him.

My Journal

Perhaps one day I will return to this world of diversity, because here we are different and can accept that, unlike in my country where the birth of equality has buried the roots of heritage.

Here we are free: we are friends, outside the realms of labels and stereotypes; we have knowledge only of what we experience and an open mind to what we have not. Perhaps there is a pattern to the madness we see and to our own. My friend I left today, never to see again, but together we fly; in spirit of the experience, we sail forever.

    ---fountain in Paris waiting for Sarah.

30. Paradise

France was too expensive for me. In Amsterdam my American dollar was worth twice as much, and I could live in the campground for fifty dollars a week. That was about all the money I had left after I bought a ticket for the train to take me there.

I was leaving Sarah again. I loved her and it scared the lights out of me. She was like owning a nice Harley. You loved the way she made you feel and couldn't keep your eyes off of her. Yet, you were constantly worried about losing her, or something happening to her. She was something precious and beautiful—the kind of lady a man would walk across a continent for.

Sarah's Journal

> Marty left this morning for Amsterdam. I will meet him on Friday. We went to see The Blair Witch Project last night. I thought it was very well done. We are starting to get used to each other. I don't know why I hate that. I need my space right now, and I feel smothered. I hate that too. I really like this

guy a lot, but I've got to breathe for awhile now, and what am I doing? I'm running off to spend yet another weekend with him in Amsterdam. I don't know if four days apart is going to satisfy our desperate needs for solitude, But I really want to go to Amsterdam. So I will go and hope that we don't get tired of each other too fast. I don't know what is going to happen when we get back to Texas. Things may completely change, and I must be ready for that. We both need to, but he keeps talking crazy: "I want to travel the world with you! We would have cool kids together!" he talks too much of things that should not be thought of right now. It's too fast. Our relationship wasn't moving fast enough for so long, and now I feel crowded. How did this happen? When and why did you start moving at warp speed, and why do I find commitment so depressing?!

When I arrived in Amsterdam my second time, Central Station was like an old friend. It was getting late and I didn't go into the city. I went out the back of Central Station to the ferry that would carry me across the canal towards Vliegenbos.

Again, the brisk climate was a good change from the heat of Paris. The mist from the swells splashing against the ferry touched my face, and I watched the big ships going out to sea. A little girl in pigtails on her mom's bicycle was smiling at me with bright, blue eyes. To her this was everyday life.

For me it was a life to be enjoyed for a short time: my paradise.

On the way to Vliegenbos, I stopped at the market for bread, cheese, potatoes and carrots. There were no Aussies in the front field. There were no Irish. The land they called Texas was now home to someone else. Vliegenbos was an ever changing environment and to be happy there, one had to learn how to adapt.

It was misting, and the grounds were even more crowded than before. I made a place inside a small hedge of trees. The brush was thick, but once inside, there was room enough to stand. There was some trash that I cleaned up where people had thrown things away into the bushes, and I trimmed a few low limbs with my big knife to make it comfortable. No one had ever thought to camp in there. It was neat, my own private spot.

Setting up my tent, I was happy as ever. The little yellow tent had become my home base and where ever I moved it was there to shelter me. I was comfortable on the ground. I hadn't slept in a bed since I left Texas. I had the things I needed and nothing more.

I rolled out my mat on the ground beside the tent and crawled inside myself to spend the evening alone—listening to the sounds of Vliegenbos.

Later, when I crawled in the tent, I found an earring that Sarah had been missing. The rest of the night I thought of her.

My Journal

Amsterdam, I'm back, things are different than before. Everything is different after the first time; if not it's only pointless repetition.

I was alone every evening this time around. Days, I also spent alone. It was peaceful and allowed me time to reflect on my travels and my future. Roaming the streets of Amsterdam and spending afternoons in Vondel Park, I took in the harmony around me. I took no seconds for granted and left no thoughts unexplored.

The greens were greener and the rhythm of life was all around. Sarah was coming to visit soon and she would see this dream I had seen.

31. Sarah

She came by train to Central Station on a Friday afternoon.

Sarah's Journal

> Oh, I just want to get off this train and find you. I miss you. I want you to hold me. I sound corny, I know, but I miss your arms around me. I just want to find you and go and sit in a coffee shop and smoke some whatever and have a coffee. Every time I think of seeing you again, I get so antsy I can hardly stand it. I can't breathe in here. The smoke is so thick, and it is so crowded. I'm beginning to love you. I can't help myself. I think, subconsciously, I've been holding back, trying to protect myself. But I'm tired now. I'm ready to fall. Please be careful with me, Marty.

She was hungry when she arrived, and beautiful. I was hungry for her. We had little time before sunset, and she wanted one of the wonderful falafels I had told her about.

My Irish friends and I had stumbled upon a great falafel stand the first time I was here. Grant had found it, and I didn't even know what a falafel was. Sarah didn't either and was excited about eating one soon.

"Come on. We'll stop by a smoke shop on the way back," I said, taking her hand and leading her across the canal that led into the city.

The city was like home to me; it had become my natural environment. I didn't think to slow down and let Sarah take it in until she lightly tugged back on my hand. I turned around to see her smiling face. She was in awe of the beauty of the city as I was the first time I walked out of Central Station.

I took the pack from her shoulders and transferred it to mine. I put my arms around her from behind. Her hair felt nice against my neck. I held her there until she took my arm, turning around to kiss me.

"I'm glad you're here," I said.

"I'm glad I'm here, too."

"Isn't it beautiful?"

"I love it."

"I love you."

"I love you, too."

She took my hand and led me into the city as if she knew where we were going.

32. The Horizon

Time with her in Amsterdam was bliss. I showed her the city, we napped in Vondel Park, and it all went by to quickly. She snapped a picture of me playing the bass in the music store with the fine Spanish guitars. We were alone with the basses and I never wanted us to leave.

My last ride on the ferry reminded me of my first and the many rides in between. I saw Grant, Maread, and Charlie sleepy eyed in the morning sun. I saw the Aussies looking at their map—and I saw myself with my guitar—the Texan who had gone on a walk-about.

Our train to Paris was scheduled for late afternoon, and my last hours in Amsterdam were bittersweet. I played a few more songs on Dam Square, in the mist, among the tourists and other street performers, pigeons on cobblestone and foot traffic all around.

Sarah was shopping, searching for something for her bookshelf at home. She returned with a gift for me: a decorative tin box for rolling tobacco. There was an image of a white wolf printed on the lid.

With tears in my eyes, I thanked her, hugging her tight so that she could not see my face...and the people around us faded away.

Sarah's Journal

Well, to set the scene...It's Monday. It's raining in Paris, and I'm sitting alone at a Tabac Café with my Coca-Cola Light, waiting for the movie, *Happiness*, to start across the street. I have about an hour's wait. You left this morning to go back to Texas. What will it be like between us once I am back? You keep many feelings to yourself; I don't like that. It's getting a little cold out here. Oh, Marty! Why did you leave me?
I wonder where You are. I miss you.

My Journal

The pilot says, "Temperature in Houston is 98 degrees, and we should be there in nine hours and 40 minutes." Holy shit! I am going home. I have no home. My home is the road. I live on the breeze, wherever it takes me, and now it takes me back to Texas. On a journey to find myself, I feel more lost than before, that is a good feeling. There are still oceans I haven't crossed and mountains I haven't climbed.
On another note, for the first time in my life, I am completely, absolutely broke; I have been since I sold everything and bought the

tickets for this adventure. I have become like Grant, always looking for a bargain. Thoughts of food rush through my head every second—and I love it.

I haven't slept in a bed, nor driven, watched TV, or enjoyed air conditioning. I have been on the road in search mainly of food. I've been sitting on the ground eating raw potatoes, cheese and bread, and drinking water because it is free—and loving it.

It kills me that I could not stay longer.

I only hope things between Sarah and I do not change back in Texas. Soon we will see. I do say this here and now: I will never love another the way I love her. There may be others, but she is the one; I know it. I already miss her dearly; already I feel empty. She makes me whole; she inspires me to do things I normally could not. She is the sweetest thing I have ever known.

I did not tell her these feelings of mine. I'm writing them now. Maybe it is for the best.

Texas

Sarah's Journal

Okay, I'm in my room alone again, except now I have wine and cigarettes. I finished my Judy Blume book last night. It was good; kind of sad. I nearly cried, but of course, I've been a little emotionally unbalanced lately. I'm late on my period and that worries me.

I can't wait to see you back in Huntsville at my apartment. I remember our last night together there. We talked about our fears of traveling and how we would find each other somehow. I miss that time. I wonder if it can be recaptured. I don't know, but what memories we have made!

I love you for the moments that we have had. You have shown me love in its purest form. I thank you for that. I can't wait to find you again so I can tell you how much I love you. No matter what happens, I will never think of Paris without thinking of you.

In Texas, I could have called my folks or friends for a ride home from the airport, but I did not—the journey was not over. Instead I walked for days in the Texas heat.

Nights I dreamt of camping with the Aussies by the mountain stream and Sarah was with me and all of my friends. Mornings turned to the hottest of hot while images of Paris, Amsterdam, and Switzerland flashed through my mind. And I kept walking like I did through Belgium—out of Houston and into beautiful Texas.

Walking down the dirt road to my house, only two miles away from where I started, I stopped. I could hear the tractors working close by. Dust covered leaves, white along the road. I stayed there for hours and no one came by because that's how far out in the country I was—again.

Sarah's Journal

It has been five days since marty left. I'm about to go to sleep now. In the morning, I'm off to the airport. Good night for the last time. Good night Bordeaux. Good night Dunhills. Good night ashtray. Good night peeling walls. Good night prison bed. Good night Seine river. Good night Paris.

Marty and Sarah were married on January 26, 2002,
in Gatlinburg, Tennessee.

Thank you, Lord, for your blessings.

Printed in the United States
125432LV00001B/92/P

9 781432 729080